D1385009

Bears can come,
Bears can go.
Bears are very nice to know.

Bears are friendly,
Bears are fun.
Bears are kind to everyone.

Good-bye!

See you in the next book.

Bears can dance,
Bears can sing.
Bears can do most anything!

Here are White Bear and
Orange Bear.
They are going for a walk.
You can see them
from the **front**.

back

front

Now they have turned around.
You can see them from the **back**.

behind

beside

in front of

These bears are in the park.
Big Bear is **behind** the tree.
Yellow Bear is **beside** the tree.
Panda Bear is asleep **in front of** the tree.

over

under

These bears are playing games.
Orange Bear is jumping **over** Black Bear.
Tiny Bear is crawling **under** Gray Bear.

The Bears are having fun.
These bears are going **up** and **down** the stairs.

up

down

Point to the bears who are going up the stairs.
How many bears are going down the stairs?

Gray Bear is standing on stilts.
The stilts make her very **tall**.

Orange Bear's trousers are **long**.
Black Bear's trousers are **short**.

tall

long

short

big

The Bears are learning that
everything has a size.
Big Bear is **big**.
Small Bear is **little**.

Some things are **tiny**.
Brown Bear and Panda Bear
have found a tiny insect.

little

tiny

What shape is Yellow Bear's kite?
Can you see a circle in the picture?
Can you see a square in the picture?
How many bears are in the boat?
What color is the boat's sail?
Can you remember the names of all the shapes?

circle

square

triangle

oblong

diamond

star

This shape is called a **diamond**.

This shape is called a **star**.

Can you point to the diamond?
Which shape is Orange Bear holding?
How many stars can you see on the page?

This shape is called an **oblong**.

What color is the oblong?
Can you see any other oblongs on the page?

This shape is called a **square**.

This shape is called a **triangle**.

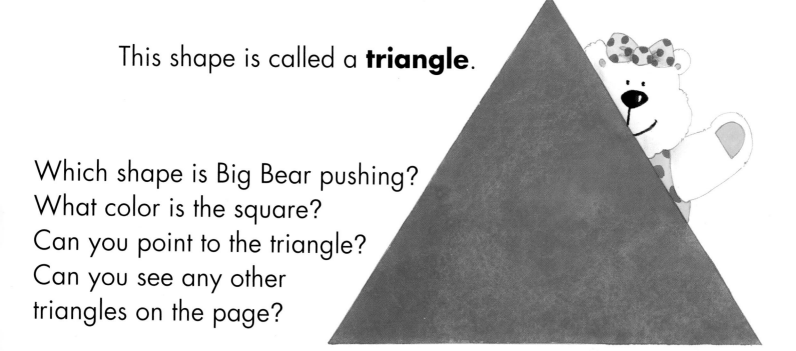

Which shape is Big Bear pushing?
What color is the square?
Can you point to the triangle?
Can you see any other
triangles on the page?

The bears are learning about shapes.
Shapes have names. Try to say the names out loud.

This shape is called a **circle**.

6
six

7
seven

8
eight

9
nine

10
ten

1 one •

2 two • •

3 three • • •

4 four • • • •

5 five • • • • •

How many bears are playing with the ball?
What color are the swings?
How many bears are in the sandbox?
Can you point to the number 5?
Can you remember all the numbers from 1 to 10?

10

10
ten kites

How many bears are sledding
down the hill?
How many kites can you see?
Can you point to the blue kites?

9
nine sleds

7
seven bikes

8
eight
umbrellas

How many bears
are jumping?

How many fish
can you see?

What color is
White Bear's bike?

Which number
comes after 7?

5
five
jumps

6
six fish

3 three hats

4 four books

The bears are learning to count.
Try to count with them. Say the numbers out loud.

1
one
drum

2
two balls

How many bears are playing a drum?
Which number comes after **1**?
How many bears are trying on hats?
How many books can you see?

The bears are having a busy day.
Some of the Bears are painting their house.
Some of the Bears are painting the fence.
What is Yellow Bear doing?
What color is Big Bear painting the gate?
Point to all the green things you can see in the picture.

yellow   blue   green   orange

black   white   gray

The Bears want to paint pictures.
Big Bear is telling them the names
of all the colors they can use.
Try to say the names of all the colors.
Which is your favorite color?

red

purple brown

Can you remember the name of
the bear who is lifting the weights?

Say hello to the Bears.

My name is Big Bear.
These are all my friends.
Turn the page to find out
their names.

What is your name?
Do you have a bear?
What is your bear called?

ONE! TWO! THREE! BEARS TEACH ME!

Written by Jenny Wood
Illustrations by Rebecca Archer

WISHING WELL BOOKS®

This book belongs to

Published by Wishing Well Books,
an imprint of Joshua Morris Publishing, Inc.,
355 Riverside Avenue, Westport, CT 06880.
Copyright © 1992 Oyster Books.
All rights reserved. Printed in Hong Kong.
ISBN: 0-88705-774-8
2 4 6 8 10 9 7 5 3

WISHING WELL BOOKS & DESIGN is a registered trademark
of The Reader's Digest Association. Inc.

Grateful thanks are due to Lizzy Pearl for her assistance
during the very early stages of this book's development,
and to Ali Brooks for her rhymes.

ONE! TWO! THREE! BEARS TEACH ME!